THE MAGIC & MYSTERY OF Trees

Written by
Jen Green

DK

DK | Penguin Random House

Author Jen Green
Illustrator Claire McElfatrick
Educational consultant Jenny Lane-Smith
Senior editor Satu Hämeenaho-Fox
Senior art editor Claire Patane
Art editor Polly Appleton
US Senior editor Shannon Beatty
Americanizer Liz Searcy
Preproduction producer Dragana Puvacic
Producer Inderjit Bhullar
Jacket designers Claire Patane,
Eleanor Bates, Jemma Westing
Jacket coordinator Isobel Walsh
Picture researcher Sakshi Saluja
Managing editor Penny Smith
Managing art editor Mabel Chan
Creative director Helen Senior
Publishing director Sarah Larter

First American edition, 2019
Published in the United States by DK Publishing
1745 Broadway, 20th Floor, New York, NY 10019

Copyright © 2019 Dorling Kindersley Limited
DK, a Division of Penguin Random House LLC
23 24 25 11 10
033–311360–Mar/2019

A catalog record for this book
is available from the Library of Congress.
ISBN 978-1-4654-7936-5

DK books are available at special discounts when purchased inbulk
for sales promotions, premiums, fund-raising, or educational use.
For details, contact: DK Publishing Special Markets,
1745 Broadway, 20th Floor, New York, NY 10019
SpecialSales@dk.com

Printed and bound in China

www.dk.com

From the deepest,
densest forests to
our local towns
and cities, trees
are all around us.

We share our
world with trees,
living side by side
with them but often
overlooking them.

Wander through the
pages of this book to
discover the secret
lives of trees.

CONTENTS

WHAT IS A TREE ?

A tree is a huge plant that towers above us. You'll find trees standing alone in people's yards or clustered together in thick forests.

Trees are true wonders of nature. Some species can grow taller than 50 cars stacked on top of each other! Trees can live for hundreds of years, and the very oldest are thousands of years old.

Every part of a tree works together. From the deepest roots that burrow through the earth, to the smallest leaf on the highest branch, every part of a tree is working hard to help it survive.

When you get to know these silent giants, you'll never look at trees the same way again...

Where in the world?

From rocky coasts to lush valleys, trees are found almost everywhere. Forests are places where many trees grow together.

Canada's most famous tree, the **maple**, produces maple syrup.

The world's tallest trees, **redwoods**, live in western North America.

North America

Broad-leaved forests grow in parts of North America and Europe with mild climates.

South America

The biggest **rain forest** in the world is the Amazon in South America. **Tropical rain forests** grow close to the equator, around the earth's middle, where it is very hot all year round.

Monkey puzzle trees grow in Chile, at the tip of South America.

N
NW   NE
W   E
SW   SE
S

KEY

Acacia
Ash
Aspen
Banyan
Baobab
Birch
Cabbage tree
Cedar
Chinese fire tree
Cocoa
Coconut palm
Date palm
Douglas fir
Elm
Eucalyptus
Fig
Golden larch
Handkerchief tree
Huasai palm
Jacaranda
Japanese beech
Juniper
Kapok
Kauri
Lime
Linden

FOREST TYPES

There are three main types of forests: **broad-leaved forests**, **conifer forests**, and **rainforests**. Each of these forests is made up of different types of trees.

A huge **conifer forest** stretches across northern North America, Russia, and northern Europe. These places have long, snowy winters.

Europe

Asia

Coconut seeds can float for miles before finding a place to grow.

Africa

Kauri pines live only in New Zealand. They can get very old and large.

Eucalyptus, or gum, trees grow in Australia's dry forests. They keep their leaves all year round.

Australasia

Forests cover almost a third of earth's dry land.

Loblolly pine | Mahogany | Mango | Mangrove | Monkey puzzle | Maple | Norway spruce | Nutmeg | Oak | Olive | Pine | Poplar | Quaking aspen | Ramon | Redwood | Red maple | Rowan | Rubber | Sacred fig | Sausage tree | Silver birch | Spruce | Sitka spruce | Strangler fig | Teak | Umbrella thorn

How trees live

You've never seen a tree eat a bowl of noodles or a peanut butter sandwich, so what do they eat? As long as it has sunlight, water, and a gas called carbon dioxide, a tree can live, grow, and even make its own food!

The amazing food-making process of plants is called photosynthesis.

Trees are tough, but they must stay warm to survive. If the water in the tree's leaves freezes, it can't make food for itself.

Mealtime

A tree's green leaves soak up light from the sun. Then they use energy from the light to mix carbon dioxide and water. This makes a sugary liquid called sap, which is the tree's food.

Summer days

Broad-leaved trees only make food in spring and summer, because there is more sunlight. They lose their leaves in the fall. Conifers can have leaves or needles. They keep making food throughout the winter.

Making oxygen

While they are busy making sap, the tree's leaves give off a gas called oxygen. All animals, including us, breathe in oxygen and breathe out carbon dioxide. If there were no plants such as trees, we wouldn't have air to breathe.

Types of trees

With so many trees growing around the world, it can be tricky to tell one leafy plant from another. Luckily, there are only two main families of trees: **broad-leaved** trees and **conifers**.

Oak leaves

Pinecone

Needles

Broad-leaved

These trees have wide, flat leaves. They all make flowers, although some are almost too small to see. Their seeds ripen inside juicy fruits, such as plums or figs. Most broad-leaved trees drop their leaves in fall and grow new ones in spring.

Conifer

These trees have long, thin leaves called needles. Many conifers are called evergreens because they keep their leaves all year round. Conifer seeds are found inside hard, bumpy cones, such as pinecones.

ROUND

Oak

The branches of a round tree spread themselves evenly upward and outward from the trunk.

BROAD

Maple

A broad tree has branches that spread farther to the sides than upward.

SPREADING

Banyan

These trees have branches that grow up and out to create a wide, flat shape.

OVAL

Hornbeam

Oval trees have a rounded shape that is taller than it is wide.

The leafy part of the tree above the trunk is called the crown. It comes in different shapes. Many broad-leaved trees are wide and round, while conifers are often shaped like cones.

WEEPING

Willow

A weeping tree has branches that droop downward.

PALM

Coconut palm

Palms are broad-leaved trees that grow in hot countries. Unlike other trees, they don't grow side branches.

TALL AND THIN

Cypress

Some trees have closely packed branches that grow upward. Many conifers are tall and thin.

CONE

Spruce

A cone-shaped tree's branches get shorter as they go up the the trunk, ending in a pointy tip.

Parts of a tree

BRANCHES

Branches grow from the trunk. They divide to form smaller branches, which end in twigs. Leaves sprout from twigs. Flowers and fruit grow from twigs at certain times of year.

CANOPY

High above the ground, twigs and leaves weave together to form a dense, dark blanket called the canopy.

Bud

In spring, buds burst open, and leaves and flowers unfurl from them.

TRUNK

The sturdy trunk grows from the ground. It is very strong and supports the weight of the tree's branches.

Bark is a thin, tough layer that covers the trunk.

STUMP

When a tree is cut down or its trunk breaks, it leaves behind a stump.

ROOTS

Underground roots hold the tree steady in the ground.

Wherever they grow, all trees have the same parts: roots, a trunk, branches, and leaves.

Secret roots

In the damp, dark world below, roots spread through the soil to form a woody network. Up to a third of the tree is hidden underground.

Cozy homes

Rabbits and tiny creatures, such as worms and beetles, live among the roots.

Holding tight

Roots have two main jobs. First, they hold the tree firmly in the ground, so it will not blow over in a storm. Second, they draw up water containing minerals from the soil, so the leaves can make food.

Reaching out

Some trees have a big main root called a **tap root**. While most roots grow sideways, the tap root shoots straight down. A tree's root network is often wider than the tree is tall, so that it can find as much water as possible.

Trees do most things slowly, but they drink very fast! A big tree can suck in over 100 gallons of water from the soil every day.

Trunk

Pollution
Tree roots are very sensitive. They can sense pollution in the soil and avoid it by growing in a different direction.

Oil spill

Water seekers
The main roots divide into smaller ones. The smallest ones at the end of the root are called **rootlets**. They are covered in fine hairs that can sense water.

Rootlets

Water travels **up** the roots.

Big and tough
The main roots are strong and woody, like branches. Each root tip has a tough cap to push through the soil as it grows. These big roots can extend into the ground up to 5 feet (1.5 m).

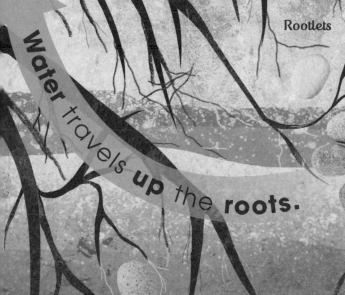

Trunk and bark

A tree's trunk supports its branches, just like your skeleton holds up your body. The trunk has to be very sturdy to support the huge weight of all the branches. **A tree simply wouldn't be a tree without a trunk!**

Inside the trunk

At the center of the trunk is the heartwood. This grew when the tree was young. It is surrounded by sapwood, which contains tiny tubes that carry water from the roots to the leaves.

Between the sapwood and the outer bark is a very thin layer called the phloem. This carries sugar from the leaves to the rest of the tree.

Phloem

Bark

Tree rings provide clues about the tree's history.

Wide rings show years when the tree grew quickly.

Narrow rings show when the tree grew only a little, because conditions were too cold or dry.

Heartwood

Sapwood

Bark, like this peeling birch bark, is the outer layer of the trunk. It stops the tree from drying out and protects it from insects and fungi.

Young trees have **smooth bark**. As trees get older, their bark cracks, peels, and becomes **more wrinkly**, like the bark of this scaly tree.

Different types of trees have different bark. Bark is also home to **lichens**, like the blotchy yellow ones here.

Try making **bark prints** by rubbing crayons onto a piece of paper placed on bark. The **texture** will come through.

17

Water pumpers

Veins are like tiny pipelines running through the leaf. They take in water from the tubes in the trunk's sapwood, and carry food made by the leaves to the rest of the tree.

Leaves

Next time you are outdoors, take a close look at a leaf. Leaves are very special, because it's in the leaves that the tree works its magic by making its own food.

Beech leaf

Veins

Light catchers

Broad-leaved trees spread their wide, flat leaves to capture as much sunlight as possible. Each leaf is like a miniature solar panel, soaking up energy from the Sun.

Leaf shapes

Each tree has leaves with a slightly different shape. They can be long and thin, or wide and round. Flat, round leaves are good at catching sunlight, but also lose more water.

Trees can't move from place to place, but they can very slowly turn their leaves to face the sun.

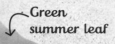
Green
summer leaf

Fading
to yellow

Dry,
brown leaf

Leaves are green
because they contain
a natural pigment
called chlorophyll.
In fall the green
fades and other
colors in the leaves
can be seen. They
turn yellow, orange,
and brown.

Turning orange
in fall

Follow one maple tree through the seasons...

SPRING

SUMMER

Buds

Green leaves

Sun and rain wake the tree from its slumber.

A full crown of leaves grows.

First shoots

After the cold, dark winter, spring is the season of new beginnings. The weather gets warmer, and days grow longer. Trees know when the winter has passed. In spring, the tree grows green buds. The buds open, uncurling and spreading new leaves in the sunshine. The tree's flowers bloom.

Hot days

Like many humans, trees love the sunshine. Summer is the hottest season, with the longest days of the year, and the trees are ready to soak up the sunlight. Branches are covered with leaves that form a dense, shady layer. In late summer, the tree's fruits start to grow. Trees do most of their growing during the summer months.

FALL

Red leaves

Leaves lose
their green
color and fall.

Changing colors
In fall, the weather turns cooler,
and days get shorter. Fruits and
nuts ripen, and trees spread their
seeds. Flat, wide leaves can
catch blustery autumn winds, so
the tree sheds them to avoid
damage to its branches. Its
green leaves turn yellow,
orange, red, and brown, then
drift down to the ground.

WINTER

No leaves

Bare branches
won't get weighed
down with snow.

Frosty flakes
Winter is the coldest season,
with the shortest days. The
tree has shed its leaves. It may
look dead, but it is only
sleeping as it waits for spring.
The tree has moved the stocks
of sap it spent all summer
making away from its
branches and into its roots.

FLOWERS, FRUITS, AND SEEDS

Trees need to make new trees for the forest to stay healthy. That's why they grow flowers, fruits, and seeds.

The flowers bloom in spring. During the warm days of spring, bees buzz from tree to tree, visiting as many flowers as they can.

Seeds are little bundles that contain a whole new tree, ready to grow. They ripen in summer and fall. Each seed needs to find a good place to grow.

Trees, like all living things, are born, grow, and eventually die. But they leave behind the promise of new forests still to come...

Left, cocoa tree pods containing seeds

Flowers

Trees that want to attract **insects** have large, showy flowers, while ones that spread pollen on the **wind** have tiny, delicate ones. Some tree flowers are so small that they can be tricky to spot, but they have vital work to do.

Blossoms

In spring, apple and cherry trees are covered with flowers we call **blossoms**. These flowers make the trees look beautiful, but their main job is to tell insects such as bees that there's a treat ready for them.

Cherry tree blossom

Did you know flowers have male and female parts? The male part produces **pollen**. The female part makes **eggs**. Male pollen must combine with these eggs to make them fertile, and then they can ripen into seeds.

Little helpers

Insects visit flowers to drink a sweet liquid called **nectar**. Any pollen grains from the flower that get on the insect's body rub off inside the next flower the bee visits. This makes the next flower fertile.

Grains of pollen stick to the bee's **hairy body**.

The bright colors and sweet smells of flowers tell the insects the nectar is ready.

Pollen

Pine and fir trees spread their pollen on the wind.

Fruits and seeds

Once the tree's flowers have been made fertile by pollen, it is **time for seeds to grow**. They can develop inside fruits, cones, hard shells, or papery covers.

Conifer seeds

Conifer seeds

Most conifer trees make their seeds inside **cones**, not fruits. When the seeds are ripe, the cones open. The light, **papery seeds** tumble out and blow away on the breeze. Yew and juniper are unusual conifers. They make small, bitter berries. Birds love them!

Cherries

Fruits

If you've ever enjoyed a crisp apple or juicy cherry, you've eaten the fruit of a broad-leaved tree. Mangoes, peaches, and cherries contain just one large seed, called a **stone**. Apples, oranges, and lemons have many small seeds called **pips**.

The hard shells on these seeds look very different, but they all do the same job. They **protect seeds** and help them spread.

Acorns

Hazel, chestnut, and walnut trees make seeds with hard shells—we call these **nuts**. Acorns are the seeds of the oak tree.

Chestnuts

Sycamore
seeds

Maple and
sycamore seeds
have a double
wing. They spin
like miniature
helicopter blades,
to land far away.

Blown on the wind

Tree seeds must be scattered far
and wide so that new trees can
grow. Some seeds are scattered
by the wind. Sycamore, maple,
and ash trees have light, **winged**
seeds that spin through the air.

Carried by currents

Trees that live by rivers and oceans
make seeds that float. The current
carries them away. **Coconut palms**
grow on the seashore in warm
places. Ripe coconuts plop into
the water. The tide washes them
away to take root on distant coasts.

Unripe, green coconuts

Coconuts are light enough to **float**.

Animal assistants

Animals love the bright colors and mouth-watering smells of fruit. Trees get animals to **spread their seeds** for them by putting them inside delicious things.

ADVENTURE TIME

For children, the best place to grow up is near our parents, who provide everything we need. Trees are very different—they like their seeds to travel alone to distant places. Fast-moving animals provide a perfect transportation system.

Buried nuts

In fall, **squirrels** and **blue jays** prepare for winter by burying nuts and acorns. These nuts provide a handy source of food during the long, bleak months of winter—as long as the animal doesn't forget where its food is buried! Any forgotten seeds will sprout into new trees in the spring.

Monkey dung

Monkeys love to feast on figs. They can digest the juicy flesh, but the hard seeds pass right through the animals' bodies and come out in their poo!

As the monkeys wander from tree to tree, the seeds in their dung get scattered all over the forest. Monkey poo contains all the nutrients a seed needs to sprout and grow strong and healthy.

Tropical fig tree

From seed to tree

Trees are the tallest living things in the world, but they are born from tiny seeds. Growing to their full height can take 100 years. Here's how a young oak sprouts from a little acorn to grow taller than a house.

Seeds are full of food to keep the seedling going until it can make its own food.

A young tree is called a seedling, or sapling.

Acorn

Root

Sprouting

If a seed lands in moist soil in a warm, light place, big changes start to happen. The seed swells, and the case splits open. A tiny root pokes down to take in water.

Getting taller

A small green shoot pushes up through the soil. Once the first leaves unfurl in the sunlight, the young plant can make its own food. A new, little tree is born.

Growing older

Humans grow during their childhood, but we stop when we become adults. **Trees are different**—they continue growing. What's more, they can live at least five times as long as we do. At **100 years old**, many trees are still youngsters!

Oak trees keep getting wider for 500 to 600 years.

Taller and wider

As the tree gets older, its upward growth slows and finally stops when it reaches **full height**. But if there is space, its branches and trunk continue getting wider. The trunk of a big, old tree grows about 1 inch (2.5 cm) wider each year.

Life after death

No living thing goes on forever. Trees can live for hundreds of years, but in the end even they grow old and die. Winds shake the dead tree until its trunk cracks, and it comes crashing to the ground.

A new home

But that's not the end of the story. A dead tree becomes a home for thousands of small creatures that like damp, dark places. Little beasts such as slugs, worms, woodlice, centipedes, insects, and spiders move in.

Centipede

Toadstool

Earwig

Earthworm

Fly agaric mushroom

Up to a third of all creatures that live in the forest like to live in, or eat, rotten wood.

Recycling nutrients

Small creatures and fungi feast on rotten wood and break it down. This allows the raw materials that formed the tree to return to the soil. These nutrients feed young trees and other plants, giving them a good start in life.

The fallen tree has left a gap in the forest canopy, allowing light to reach the ground. This helps seedlings flourish. Sometimes a seedling will even sprout from a log.

Brown garden snail

Garden spider

Centipede

Moss, ferns, and flowers take root in the squishy, nutritious wood of rotten logs and tree stumps. Fungi spread their threads through the damp wood, and mushrooms sprout from the trunk.

Common garden slug

Ground beetle

Woodlice

Beetles lay their eggs under the bark. When the grubs hatch, they feed on the rotten wood.

TREE PARTNERS

Trees grow and change so slowly that it's hard to tell how busy they really are. Year after year, trees stand still and silent, but there's a lot going on under the surface.

Trees are mysterious things. Recently, scientists have found out that the trees in a forest work together. They make friends and support one another. Trees look after their neighbors, and mother trees pass food to their children and older trees within the family.

We now know trees have senses. They can smell, taste, touch, and feel pain, like we do. Trees can sense danger and defend themselves against enemies. **We are learning that there's a lot more to trees than we ever imagined.**

Living together

Life in the natural world is tough. It's easier for trees to survive when they help one another. Trees living in a forest grow best if all the trees are healthy. If one tree is in trouble, the others help it. Trees also work together to make the forest warmer and more sheltered in winter, and cooler, damper, and shadier in summer.

Family and friends

Trees of the same species look after one another. Oak, beech, and spruce trees like to share water and food with only their own kind. But in some places, trees of different types look out for one another too.

Stronger together

Trees grow wider until they reach the next tree. This creates a roof of branches and leaves that protects the forest from storms. If too many trees die and leave gaps, strong winds can enter and wreck the forest.

If a tree is damaged and starts to die, its neighbors will pass it food to keep it alive.

Roots

Roots spread through the soil to form a hidden web. Forest neighbors stay in touch with one another and pass food to each other through their roots.

Wood wide web

Trees like to keep in touch with each other. Experts have found out that it's not just **roots** that link the trees in a forest. They are also connected through **fungi**—the living things we know as mushrooms.

Paper birch

Hyphae

Helpful fungi like these are called **mycorrhizae** (pronounced my-cor-riz-ee).

The fungal network

Fungi are sort of like plants, but they cannot make their own food. Instead, they make a network of threads called **hyphae** (pronounced hi-fee), which break down food. The hyphae can swap food, water, and even messages with tree roots

Fungi help trees by cleaning up pollution and warding off other types of fungi that would make the trees sick.

Mushrooms and toadstools are the fruits of the fungus.

Fungus

Douglas fir

Nutrients

Food and water

Tree roots

In return for the fungal network, trees give **water** and **food** to the fungi.

Forest family

Trees of the same species act like a family. When a seedling is struggling, its mother steps in to help. Trees that are very old or damaged are not forgotten. Even the strongest trees can be attacked by disease or insects and need help every now and then. By helping each other, the trees make sure the forest as a whole stays strong.

Tiny seedling

CARING MOTHERS

Full-grown trees take care of younger and older trees. Many young trees sprout directly below the mother tree. But the youngsters don't grow well in her shade. The mother keeps them alive by passing them sap and nutrients until they are tall enough to find the light.

Older trees often block light from reaching younger ones. Far from damaging them, however, it turns out to be helpful, because growing slowly when they are young helps trees live longer.

Helping hand

This stump can't make food without leaves, but somehow it is still alive. The trees of the forest are feeding the old stump through their roots. This stump might even be the full-grown tree's mother.

Stumps can live for hundreds of years without leaves.

Tree senses

A tree doesn't have eyes, ears, fingers, or toes. Because they're so different from us, for a long time no one knew trees had senses. But now we know that they can tell what's going on around them.

They can sense the outside world...

HOT AND COLD

Trees can sense how hot or cold it is. Even tiny seeds know if the temperature has become warm enough for them to sprout and start growing.

TASTE

When an animal nibbles on a leaf, the tree can taste the animal's spit! Trees can even tell different animals apart from the taste of their spit.

TOUCH

Tree roots are amazingly sensitive. A tree can tell which roots in the underground tangle are its own. It can also tell whether its neighbors are the same type of tree.

HEARING

Roots can hear the sound of running water and grow toward it. Even when the tree is completely sealed off, it knows the water is there. We don't yet know how they do this.

We are only just beginning to uncover all the mysteries of what trees can sense.

SEEING

They may not have eyes, but trees can certainly sense light and grow toward it. Every leaf on a tree can tell which direction the light is coming from. After all, they need light to make food.

TIME

Trees live life in the slow lane, but they do keep track of time. In spring, trees can sense the days getting longer. In fall, they know the days are shorter and prepare for winter.

...and even talk back.

BEING THEMSELVES

No two trees are exactly the same. Different trees living in the same conditions will still grow into different shapes. Some trees take part in the wood wide web, while others are loners.

TALKING

Trees can talk to insects using sights and smells. The bright colors and sweet scents of flowers tell bees and butterflies that food is available.

SHOUTING

When they get thirsty, trees start yelling! If water can't flow from the roots to the leaves, the trunk starts to vibrate. That's a tree's way of complaining.

The **handkerchief tree** from China has flowers that look like dangling napkins.

Scientists are beginning to research how trees "think," using their roots like a brain.

Tree defenses

Imagine if you were a tree and an insect started to nibble on you. Ouch! Luckily, trees have lots of clever ways to stop insect invaders.

Lodgepole pine beetle

Sticky sap

Beetles attacking **lodgepole pines** often find themselves in a sticky situation! Before the yummy bark can be devoured, the pine tree imprisons the insect in a very sticky **sap trap**.

Bitter dinner

Beech, oak, and spruce trees can pump chemicals called **tannins** into their leaves to make them taste bitter. This spoils the insects' meal, so they move on to other trees.

A tree can tell what kind of bug is biting it and can send for the right helpers.

Oak leaf roller moth caterpillar

Insects to the rescue

Some trees use a different tactic to defend themselves against sap-sucking insects called **aphids**. They give off a special scent that calls **ladybugs**. These spotted insects hunt aphids and will eat them all day if they get the chance.

Ladybug eating an aphid

Acacia
thorns

Under attack

Giraffes are the natural enemies of the acacia tree. Luckily for the acacias, they have some clever defenses at the ready. Not only do they protect themselves, they also **warn other trees** of the danger.

Danger!

Acacia trees can sense giraffe spit. When the tree's leaves are being nibbled, it starts making chemicals that make the leaves taste bitter. Yuck!

Beware giraffes
Acacias have long, sharp thorns to ward off animals, but the giraffe's long, flexible tongue dodges the thorns to pluck tufts of green leaves.

Umbrella trees
Acacias are shaped like umbrellas! This is because quick giraffes gradually eat all their lower leaves.

Deterred
Giraffes don't like the bitter leaves, so they move on to other trees.

Heads up
As well as protecting themselves, the acacias give off a special scent that warns trees nearby that hungry giraffes are around.

Group effort
The acacia's neighbors pick up the scent and start making their own bitter chemicals. The giraffes now have to walk a long way to find leaves that don't taste awful.

Incredible trees

Trees are the biggest, heaviest, and oldest living things on the planet. They can live in the snowy heights of the Andes and even clone themselves.

Tallest *tree*

Biggest *tree*

Widest *tree*

Oldest *tree*

The world's very tallest tree is a **redwood** growing in California. Named Hyperion, it soars 377 feet (115 m) high—the height of about 20 giraffes!

A **giant sequoia** named General Sherman is the world's largest individual living thing. It has a massive trunk 26 feet (8 m) across.

A **Montezuma bald cypress** called the Tule Tree stands in a churchyard in Mexico. It is the world's widest tree and measures 119 feet (36 m) around the trunk but is only 116 feet (35 m) tall.

The world's oldest known tree is a **bristlecone pine** named Methusela. It grows high in the White Mountains of California and is 4,800 years old.

Trees can live for a long time in all kinds of places because they are good at adapting to different environments.

Highest tree

Heaviest tree

Oldest roots

The roots of a **Huon pine** growing in Tasmania, Australia, are an epic 10,500 years old.

A group of **quaking aspen** trees in a forest in Utah are all identical sprouts of one tree, connected by roots. This makes the group the world's heaviest living thing. Together the trees weigh as much as 33 blue whales.

The tough **Polylepis** trees of South America can grow at heights of up to 17,000 feet (5,200 m) in the Andes Mountains, where it's too cold and windy for other trees to grow.

TREE HABITATS

Trees aren't that fussy about where they live. All they need is sunshine, water, and a little soil in which to spread their roots. That's why forests are found all over the world, and why such an amazing array of animal and plant life is found within their depths.

Trees are tough survivors. Scattered trees can take root on steep, stony mountains. They cling to life on storm-battered coasts and survive howling winds in the snowy tundra. They survive on the edges of dusty deserts and on busy streets in city centers. In fact, trees can get by almost anywhere.

This section explores habitats the world over. Read on to discover how trees provide a home for an incredible variety of mammals, birds, insects, and fish.

Tree homes

This great big oak tree is home to lots of creatures. From the topmost branches to the deepest roots, animals and plants live side by side, just like people in an apartment building.

Dig in!
An old tree like this provides food for everyone—sort of like a natural **supermarket**.

Carnivores, such as **owls and bats**, are keeping a look out for small animals and insects to hunt.

Herbivores, such as insects, birds, and deer, munch on every part of the tree. They nibble on its leaves, buds, fruits, and even bark.

Below ground, in the tree's basement, **worms**, **beetles**, and **fungi** feast among the roots.

Blackbirds build cozy nests high in the branches to lay their eggs. The nests keep the chicks warm and safe from **predators** such as foxes.

This **woodpecker** drums holes in the bark with its supersharp beak to find juicy grubs. Then it slurps up the insects with its sticky tongue.

In fall, **squirrels** bury nuts in the ground to save for winter.

Foxes use their sharp claws to dig snug **dens** among the tree's roots.

Tropical rain forest

The steamy Amazon rain forest is home to more living things than any other place in the world. A small patch of rain forest can contain hundreds of types of trees.

EMERGENT

Tall trees called emergents poke their heads above the forest canopy. They can enjoy the sun without having to compete with other trees for light.

CANOPY

Rain forest trees love the hot, steamy weather. They grow tall, creating a dense, shady roof called a canopy.

Blue morpho butterfly

Kapok trees are common in the rain forest. They can grow up to 230 feet (70 m) tall.

Creeping vine

Bold beaks
Toucans have brightly colored beaks up to 7.5 inches (19 cm) long.

Green-winged macaw

Red-billed scythebill

Long limbs
Spider monkeys swing through the trees using their long arms, legs, and tails.

Anaconda

Centipede

Pitcher

Golden dart frog

Tarantula

Purple harlequin toad

Two-toed sloth

Epiphyte

At home on a tree
Epiphytes are plants that grow on other plants. Rain forest trees support many epiphytes.

Stealthy cat
The jaguar's spots help it hide among the speckled shadows cast by the leaves above. It slinks through the trees as it hunts.

Emerald tree boa

Bromeliad

Pygmy marmoset

Palm

Hoatzin

UNDERSTORY
The understory is dim because the canopy above blocks most of the light.

FOREST FLOOR
The ground level in a rain forest is dark and dry because the higher levels absorb almost all the light and rain.

Giant anteater

Temperate rain forest

Unlike tropical forests, **temperate rain forests grow in areas of mild weather**, where it is neither too hot nor too cold. Many of the trees are conifers. This misty forest is home to lots of animals that like to keep cool.

River beavers
Beavers build dams across forest streams. They gnaw through **saplings** (young trees) with their sharp front teeth. Timber! The tree crashes down to become part of the dam.

Giant redwood

Fireweed

Big cats
Pumas are large cats that silently slink through the forest. They pounce on animals as large as deer and kill them by biting their necks.

Western skunk cabbage

Tree frogs
Pacific tree frogs live in forest ponds and damp ditches. They are brown, gray, or green but can **change color** to blend in with their surroundings.

Feel of the forest

The world's largest temperate rain forest grows along the west coast of North America. It is made up mostly of **conifers**, including the tallest trees in the world, giant redwoods. The trees grow so well because they have plenty of water. The rain is heaviest in winter, but in the summer months **thick**, **damp fogs** roll in from the ocean.

Gentle giants

Moose are the largest type of deer. Males have **huge antlers**. They glide among the trees, munching ferns, grass, twigs, and tree bark.

Oregon grape

Chipmunks

Chipmunks are nimble little rodents that scamper through the forest searching for nuts, fruits, and seeds. They carry food back to their burrows in their bulging **cheek pouches**.

Raccoons

This scrappy mammal has a broad black stripe across its eyes, like a **bandit's mask**. It acts like a bandit too, raiding birds' nests to steal eggs.

Rhododendron

Swamp forest

In the hot and humid swamp, unusual trees called mangroves grow in slow-moving, murky water. In this coastal tropical forest, the trees are washed twice a day by salty tides.

Proboscis monkey

TREES ON STILTS

Mangrove trees have tall roots that lift the tree high above the water. These roots filter out most of the salt, so the tree can drink fresh water.

Sundari mangroves

Male fiddler crab

The **saltwater crocodile** lurks in gloom, waiting for prey. The muddy water around the mangrove roots is the perfect hiding place for the world's largest reptile.

Falling leaves get snapped up by crabs.

Some mangroves move salt into their leaves, which then fall off.

Buffy fish owl

The Sundarbans in Bangladesh is the world's largest mangrove forest.

Black-capped kingfisher

The **Bengal tiger** prowls the swamp in search of deer. Its striped coat provides the perfect camouflage in the tall reeds at the water's edge.

Mudskippers are strange fish that can live out of water. They skitter over the mud using their strong front fins.

Many fish hide **among the roots.**

The mangrove's roots poke into the mud and slow down the water. This stops the coast from **eroding** (wearing away) over time.

A ghostly **great gray owl** flies silently above the forest, keeping an eye out for signs of prey on the ground below.

Spruce

Larch

The **crossbill** has a pincer-shaped beak with overlapping tips. It pries open pinecones to get at the seeds inside.

Bears use their sharp claws to climb trees and get at bees' nests. The bear breaks open the nest and slurps the honey.

Red crossbill

Bear

The male **moose** has huge, branching antlers, which it likes to scratch against trees.

Snow forest

The dense, dark, **taiga** forest is covered with snow in winter. It grows across Canada, Russia, and northern Europe, wrapping itself around the world like an enormous green scarf.

Cool conifers

The taiga is made up mostly of **conifers** such as spruce and fir. Conifers' pointy shape and waxy, needle-like leaves help them shed the heavy snow.

The **taiga** covers more of the world than any other forest.

Reindeer spend the winter in these sheltered forests, eating lichens from branches and underneath the snow.

Silver birch

Reindeer

Pine martens dart along the snowy forest floor, sniffing out small animals to hunt.

Mountain hare

White world

Northern forests have short, cool summers and long, harsh winters. Snow often covers the ground for months on end.

Extreme survivors

Most trees prefer to live in mild, warm, and sunny places. However, some hardy trees can cope with incredibly **tough conditions**, such as extreme **heat** or **cold**, or long, dry periods, called droughts.

On the edge

Pine and cypress trees can grow on very windy cliffs. Powerful gusts break off branches, leaving only one side of the tree to grow. You can tell which way the winds blow by looking at these trees.

Dwarf willow

Beyond the northern taiga lies the frozen Arctic tundra. The shrublike Arctic willow can cope with the bitter cold and deep snow. It hugs the ground, out of reach of whistling winds, and takes 100 years to grow just 8 inches (20 cm) tall.

Trees love drinking water, but some have adapted to very dry environments. They snatch up every drop they can find.

Koalas don't get much nutrition from eucalyptus leaves, so they save energy by sleeping for up to 18 hours a day.

Koala home

Tall eucalyptus, or gum, trees grow in dry areas of Australia. Koalas will eat only eucalyptus leaves.

Water tank

Baobab trees grow on the dry, grassy plains of Africa. In the rainy season, baobabs store water in their trunks to survive the dry season.

Fireproof

Ponderosa pine trees can survive fires. They have extra-thick protective bark that can grow up to 4 inches (10 cm) thick.

TREES AND ME

Trees help us in a hundred different ways. They provide food, wood, and many other useful products. They make the air fresh and healthy by creating oxygen and help make our planet a clean place to live.

Trees take good care of us and other living things. Yet all over the world, people are harming trees. We cut forests down for timber and to make room for farms and cities. We also cause pollution that is hurting trees.

Trees do a lot to keep our world green and healthy. They provide a home for the countless plants, animals, and people who live in forests around the world. In turn, it's up to each and every one of us to take good care of trees.

Ice cream

Junk food

Palm tree oil is used to make **pizza**, **cookies**, and **ice cream**. Rainforests are being destroyed to make space for the trees that create the oil. To protect the rainforests, it's best not to eat too many treats made with palm oil.

Pizza

Cookies

Mango

Peaches

Pears

Avocados

Fruit salad

Fruit trees once grew wild in forests, but now they are grown mainly by humans in **orchards** or **plantations**. We eat the seeds inside some fruits, such as pomegranates.

Orange

Apricots

Pomegranate

Figs

Dates

Sweet, sticky **dates** come from the date palm.

Cherries

Harvest time

From a piece of juicy fruit to spicy guacamole, trees provide us with so many mouth-watering meals. Without trees, there would be no chocolate, mango yogurt, or avocado toast! They even produce powerful medicines that help us get well when we're feeling ill.

Apples

Almonds

Crunchy nuts
Lots of nuts come from trees, including brazil nuts, which come from one of the tallest trees in the Amazon rainforest. Coconut palms produce the largest nuts of any tree.

Aspirin

Tree doctor
The headache medicine aspirin originally comes from the bark of the willow tree. Another helpful tree is the cinchona, which creates a medicine called quinine that helps treat malaria.

Cashews

Brazils

Plums

Coconut

Cinnamon bun

Spicy flavors
Without trees, our food would be very bland. Cinnamon and nutmeg can really spice up a meal! Kola nuts are used to flavor fizzy cola. Beans from the cacao tree give chocolate its unique taste.

Cola

Nutmeg spice on a custard tart

Chewing gum
Sap from the chicle tree is used to make rubbery chewing gum.

Maple syrup

Chocolate

Sweet syrup
The maple syrup on your pancakes is made from the sap of the sugar maple. It is collected by hammering a metal tap into the tree's trunk and catching the sap that drips out.

Paper goods

Paper and cardboard are made from tiny chips of soft wood mixed with water. This makes a mushy pulp, which is then rolled flat and dried.

Wooden world

Take a look around your home. How many objects can you find that are made of wood? From pencils made from cedar to pine furniture, wood is all around the home.

It takes **at least 30 years** to grow a pine tree for wood.

Made from trees

Wood is a super-material. It's strong, beautiful, and can be grown in an eco-friendly way. We use this incredible material to build our houses and to make all kinds of objects.

The bark of cork trees is used to make bulletin boards, corks for wine bottles, and place mats. It's so light it can float!

Hardy wood

Trees such as oak and maple make strong hardwood that is used for roof beams and furniture. Tropical hardwoods such as mahogany and rosewood are used to make guitars because they create a clear sound. Hardwood is strong and tough, but the trees grow very slowly.

Rubber

Rubber trees ooze a milky sap, which is turned into car and bicycle tires. Rubber boots, party balloons, and rubber bands are also made from rubber.

A type of incense called agarwood, which comes from aquilaria trees, is worth more than gold!

Trees and the planet

Trees are vital to every single person on the planet. They keep the earth cool and moist, which makes it a nice place to live. Trees love to soak up water, but don't worry. They are willing to share it with the rest of us. They even help to create clouds. This process is called the water cycle.

Leaves catch rain and give off extra moisture the tree doesn't need as water vapor.

THE WATER CYCLE

Water moves between the sea, air, and land in a nonstop cycle called the water cycle. Trees play a very important part in this. By releasing water back into the air, and absorbing it through their roots, they stop rain from flowing right back into the sea.

Water rises from the ocean as a gas called water vapor.

Forests help cool the air around the earth. The planet is already warmer than it should be, but without trees it would heat up even more.

High in the air, the moisture from the trees forms clouds.

When clouds float over high areas such as mountains, water falls as rain or snow.

Rain

The clouds move inland, bringing rain to places that would be dry without it. Without trees, deserts would cover much more of the earth.

The water flows back down toward lower ground.

River

Any rain that the trees don't absorb soaks into the soil or runs off into rivers.

Trees at risk

All over the world, people are cutting down trees to use the land covered by forests. Slowly but surely, even vast forests like the Amazon are getting smaller. We also harm trees by spreading pollution. We need to take better care of our precious forests.

FOREST DESTRUCTION

Why are forests disappearing?
People cut down trees for timber and also to light wood fires to keep warm and to cook. We clear forest land to build new roads and cities and to make way for new farms and ranches, where we raise cattle and grow crops.

Lost homes
When the loggers move in, the whine of chainsaws fills the air. Mighty trees come crashing down. Logs are loaded onto trucks. In the end, all that is left are broken stumps. Animals such as birds and deer run for their lives and are left with nowhere to live. This is called habitat destruction.

Effects

Tree roots keep the soil together. Without trees to slow down and suck up the rain, the water washes soil into rivers. This can cause flooding. Eventually, the whole area becomes drier, so farmers find it harder to grow crops.

Pollution

Cars, factories, and power plants in faraway cities can harm trees. They give off smoke and fumes that drift on the wind to pollute distant forests. The pollution makes trees drop their leaves, so they get sick and eventually die.

Helping trees

Trees deserve our love and care. After all, they do a lot to keep our world healthy. In turn, it's up to all of us to take better care of the world's trees. We can use recycled paper, or even plant a new tree.

PLANT A TREE

Make space in your garden, park, or other open space for a brand new tree. Buy a young tree (sapling) and make a home for it to grow.

Shovel

Sapling

Dig

Dig a deep hole in the ground. Make sure the hole is twice as wide as the roots of the tree and the same depth. Different trees like different soil, but most like loose, moist ground where their roots can grow.

Plant

Plant a sapling that you have bought from a plant nursery. Put a piece of wood across the soil around the top of the tree's roots. This will show you where the roots come up to. They should be just at ground level.

Some forests, such as national parks and reserves, are protected. Workers called foresters look after the trees and plant ones when needed.

Stake

Fill
Shovel earth into the hole, making sure it is not packed in too tightly. The sapling's roots should be completely covered but with room to grow. Tie the tree to a stake to help it stand up in the wind.

Water
Water your tree to give it the best chance to grow. Remove any weeds around it, and keep an eye out for pests. In two to three years, you'll be able to remove the stake, and your tree will stand proud on its own.

National and state trees

Different species of trees thrive in different parts of the world. People grow to love the trees they see around them as they grow up. Over time, a particular tree can become connected with a region. Many of the world's people love one tree so much they want it to represent them and have made it their **national or state tree.**

(U) = unofficial

Afghanistan Mulberry (U)
Albania Olive
Algeria Date palm (U)
Andorra Pyrenean willow (U)
Angola Mangrove (U)
Anguilla White cedar
Antigua and Barbuda Whitewood
Argentina Jacaranda
Aruba (Netherlands) Divi-divi (windblown tree) (U)
Australia Eucalyptus (gum tree)
Azerbaijan Iberian oak
Bahamas Lignum vitae
Bahrain Thorn tree (U)
Bangladesh Mango
Barbados Bearded fig tree
Belarus Birch (U)
Belize Mahogany
Benin Palm
Bermuda Bermuda cedar
Bhutan Bhutan cypress
Bolivia Breadfruit (U)
Botswana Baobab (U)
Brazil Tabebuia (Ipe-amarelo)
Brunei Mangrove (U)
Bulgaria Oak (U)
Cambodia Palmyra palm
Canada Maple
Cayman Islands Silver thatch palm

Central African Republic Baobab
Chile Monkey puzzle tree
China Chinese pine
Colombia Wax palm
Comoros Ylang-ylang (U)
Cook Islands (New Zealand) Flame tree (U)
Costa Rica Guanacaste
Croatia Beech (U)
Cuba Royal palm
Cyprus Cypriot oak
Czech Republic/Czechia Lime
Denmark Beech
Dominica Banana and palm
Dominican Republic Mahogany
El Salvador Maquilishuat
Equatorial Guinea Kapok
Eritrea Olive (U)
Estonia Oak (U)
Fiji Coconut palm (U)
Finland Silver birch
France Yew
Gabon Torchwood
Gambia Oil palm
Georgia Tree of Life (U)
Germany Oak (U)
Ghana Cacao
Greece Laurel
Grenada Banana

Guadeloupe (France) Nance (U)
Guatemala Ceiba
Guinea-Bissau King palm
Haiti Breadfruit (U)
Honduras Honduran pine
Hong Kong (China) Bauhinia orchid tree
Hungary Hungarian lilac (U)
India Banyan
Ireland Sessile oak
Israel Olive
Italy Oak and olive
Ivory Coast Palm (U)
Jamaica Blue mahoe
Japan Cherry
Kiribati Breadfruit
Kuwait Royal palm (U)
Laos Dok champa
Latvia Oak and linden
Lebanon Lebanon cedar
Liberia Palm
Lithuania Oak (U)
Macedonia Macedonian pine (U)
Madagascar Traveler's tree
Malawi Mulanje cedar
Malaysia Rose hibiscus
Maldives Coconut palm
Malta Gharghar
Marshall Islands Palm
Mauritania Palm (U)

Mauritius Earring tree
Mayotte Ylang-ylang (U)
Mexico Montezuma
bald cypress (U)
Micronesia Coconut palm
Moldova Oak
Montserrat (UK) Calabash
Morocco Argan tree (U)
Mozambique African blackwood (U)
Myanmar/Burma Rosewood
Namibia Acacia (U)
Netherlands Elm (U)
New Zealand Kauri
Nicaragua Madrono
Nigeria Albizia (U)
North Korea Ginkgo
Norway Norway spruce (U)
Pakistan Deodar cedar
Palau Temple tree
Panama Panama tree
Papua New Guinea Strangler
fig (U)
Paraguay Lapacho
Peru Cinchona
Philippines Narra (rosewood)
Poland Weeping willow
Portugal Olive and cork oak
Puerto Rico (US) Kapok
Romania Oak (U)
Russia Birch
Rwanda Acacia (U)
Saint Kitts and Nevis Coconut
palm
Saint Lucia Calabash
**Saint Vincent's and the
Grenadines** Breadfruit and
soufriere tree (both U)
Samoa Coconut palm
Sao Tome and Principe
Coconut palm
Saudi Arabia Phoenix palm
Senegal Baobab
Serbia Oak and serbian spruce
Seychelles Coco-de-mer palm
Sierra Leone Coconut palm
Slovakia Small-leaved lime
Slovenia Tilia (lime/linden)
South Africa Real yellowwood
Sri Lanka Ironwood

Sudan Palm
Suriname Suriname cherry (U)
Sweden Ornäs birch
Switzerland Murten lime (U)
Taiwan Camphor tree (U)
Tanzania African blackwood
Thailand Golden rain tree
Trinidad and Tobago Palm tree
Turkey Fig (U)
Turks and Caicos (UK)
Caicos pine
Ukraine Viburnum and willow
United Arab Emirates Date palm
United States of America Oak
Uruguay Yellow poinciana
Uzbekistan Plane tree (U)
Venezuela Araguaney
United Kingdom Oak (England),
Scots pine (Scotland),
Sessile oak (Wales)
US Virgin Islands (US) Yellow
cedar
Yemen Coffee tree
Zambia Mofu mahogany (U)
Zimbabwe Baobab (U)

UNITED STATES OF AMERICA STATE TREES

Each state of the US is represented
by an official state tree.

Alabama Southern longleaf pine
Alaska Sitka spruce
Arizona Paloverde
Arkansas Pine
California California redwood
Colorado Colorado blue spruce
Connecticut White oak
Delaware American holly
Florida Sabal palmetto
Georgia Live oak
Hawaii Kukui
Idaho Western white pine
Illinois White oak

Indiana Tulip tree
Iowa Oak
Kansas Cottonwood
Kentucky Tulip tree
Louisiana Bald cypress
Maine White pine
Maryland White oak
Massachusetts American elm
Michigan White pine
Minnesota Red pine
Mississippi Magnolia
Missouri Flowering dogwood
Montana Ponderosa pine
Nebraska Cottonwood
Nevada Single-leaf pinyon and
bristlecone pine
New Hampshire White birch
New Jersey Red oak
New Mexico Two-needle pinyon
New York Sugar maple
North Carolina Pine
North Dakota American elm
Ohio Ohio Buckeye
Oklahoma Redbud
Oregon Douglas fir
Pennsylvania Eastern hemlock
Rhode Island Red maple
South Carolina Sabal palmetto
South Dakota Black Hills spruce
Tennessee Tulip tree and eastern
red cedar
Texas Pecan
Utah Quaking aspen
Vermont Sugar maple
Virginia Flowering dogwood
Washington Western hemlock
West Virginia Sugar maple
Wisconsin Sugar maple
Wyoming Cottonwood

Glossary

BROAD-LEAVED
Tree with wide, flat leaves. Broad-leaved trees produce fruit containing seeds.

CARBON DIOXIDE
Gas in the air, which plants use to make food.

CHLOROPHYLL
Green color in a tree's leaves, which absorbs (takes in) sunlight.

CLONE
Identical copy of an animal or plant.

CONIFER
Type of tree that produces cones containing seeds.

CROWN
Leafy part of a tree.

DROUGHT
Long period without rain.

EQUATOR
Imaginary circle around the earth's middle.

FERTILE
When a plant or animal is able to have young. Trees make seeds when their flowers become fertile.

FUNGUS
Group of living things that includes mushrooms, toadstools, and molds. The plural of fungus is fungi.

GRUB
Young insect that looks like a worm.

HABITAT
Natural home of plants or animals, such as a forest or meadow.

HEARTWOOD
Wood at the center of a tree trunk, which grew when the tree was young.

HYPHAE
Tiny, branching threads that allow a fungus to feed.

MANGROVE
Tree that grows in a coastal swamp.

MINERALS
Natural substances that plants get from the soil.

NECTAR
Sugary liquid produced by flowers to attract insects.

NUTRIENTS
Nourishment. Plants get nutrients from the soil.

OXYGEN
Gas in the air, which all living things need to live.

PHLOEM
Layer under a tree's bark that transports food.

PHOTOSYNTHESIS
Process by which leaves turn sunlight and carbon dioxide into food and oxygen.

POLLEN
Tiny grains that combine with a plant's eggs so it can make seeds.

PREDATOR
Animal that hunts other animals for food. Also called a carnivore.

PREY
Animal that is hunted for food by other animals.

REPRODUCTION
When plants or animals have young.

ROOTLET
Tiny root covered with fine hairs.

SAPWOOD
Outer rings of wood in a tree trunk, which have grown in the last few years.

SEED
Part of a plant that is able to grow into a new plant.

SEEDLING
Young plant or tree.

TAPROOT
Tree's main root, which grows straight down into the soil.

VEINS
Tubes that carry water around a leaf and help it keep its shape.

Index

Acknowledgments

The publisher would like to thank the following people for their assistance: Hélène Hilton, Jolyon Goddard, Katie Lawrence, Clare Lloyd, and Abigail Luscombe for editorial help; Kitty Glavin and Eleanor Bates for design help; Helen Peters for the index; Akash Jain for picture research; and Tom Morse for CTS help.

PICTURE CREDITS

The publisher would like to thank the following for their kind permission to reproduce their photographs: (Key: a-above; b-below/bottom; c-center; f-far; l-left; r-right; t-top)

1 123RF.com: alein (cl); Eric Isselee / Isselee (bc). Dorling Kindersley: Paradise Park, Cornwall (tr). 2-3 Dreamstime. com: Designprintck. 4-5 Alamy Stock Photo: Carolyn Clarke. 5 Dreamstime.com: Designprintck. 6 123RF.com: Maksym Bondarchuk (cla, c); joseelias (cb/Rubber tree); Jat306 Jaturon Ruaysoongnern (cb/Mahogany Tree, cb, bc); fotoplanner (cla/Young birches); Smileus (fbl). Dreamstime. com: Pablo Caridad / Elnavegante (tr). iStockphoto.com: tiler84 (bc/Fig tree). 6-7 Dreamstime.com: Designprintck (b/ Background); Ruslan Nassyrov / Ruslanchik (Background). 7 123RF.com: Maksym Bondarchuk (c); Valentyn Volkov (fcl); Cherdchai Chaivimol (ca/Bodhi Tree); marigranula (c/Date palm); liligraphie (cla); fotoplanner (ca); Jat306 Jaturon Ruaysoongnern (crb, fbl). Dorling Kindersley: Lindsey Stock and Lindsey Stock (cra). Dreamstime.com: Lano Angelo / Dina83 (fcl/Baobab tree). iStockphoto.com: tiler84 (cla/ Common Fig tree). 8 123RF.com: fotoplanner (bc). Dreamstime.com: Alexander Potapov (br). 9 123RF.com: belchonock (br). Dorling Kindersley: (bl); Ian Cuppleditch (t). Dreamstime.com: Alexander Potapov (bc). 10 123RF. com: liligraphie (fcl). Dorling Kindersley: E. J. Peiker (c). Dreamstime.com: Mikelane45 (cr). 11 Dreamstime.com: Designprintck (Background). 12 123RF.com: alein (ca/ Woodpecker); Roman Iegoshyn (tr); Eric Isselee / isselee (cra). Dorling Kindersley: Alan Murphy (cb); RHS Wisley (Crabapple); E. J. Peiker (cla, cb/Owl); Paradise Park, Cornwall (ca/Bluebird). Dreamstime.com: Mikelane45 (ca). 13 123RF.com: wklzzz (cl). 14 Dorling Kindersley: Paolo Mazzei (ca). 15 Dorling Kindersley: Barrie Watts (ca); Stephen Oliver (fcla). 16 Getty Images: Don Mason (b). 17 Alamy Stock Photo: Rolf Nussbaumer Photography (c); Snap Decision (l); Colin Varndell (r). Dreamstime.com: Designprintck (Paper). 19 123RF.com: Christian Mueringer. Dreamstime.com: Designprintck (Background). 20 123RF. com: Agata Gładykowska (cla); Roman Iegoshyn (bc). Dorling Kindersley: Batsford Garden Centre and Arboretum (bl); Natural History Museum, London (br). Dreamstime.com: Jessamine (ca). 21 123RF.com: bmf2218 (tl, tc, cla). Alamy Stock Photo: WILDLIFE GmbH (clb/Norway Maple Leaf). Dorling Kindersley: Jerry Young (cb). Dreamstime.com: Motorolka (clb). Fotolia: Eric Isselee (cl). PunchStock: Corbis (fcl). 22-23 123RF.com: ammit. 23 Dreamstime.com: Designprintck (Background). 24 Dorling Kindersley: Alan Buckingham (cb). 25 Dorling Kindersley: Alan Buckingham (cr); Jerry Young (ca). 26 Dreamstime.com: Tamara Kulikova / Tamara_k (fbl). 27 Dreamstime.com: Alex Bramwell / Spanishalex (bl). 28 123RF.com: M Schaefer (bl). Dreamstime.com: Dule964 (b/Leaves); Isselee (bc). Fotolia: Steve Byland (cr). Getty Images: Paul E Tessier / Photodisc (clb). 29 123RF.com: Eric Isselee (cb, cra). Alamy Stock Photo: Duncan McKay (cl). 30 123RF.com: madllen (cb). Dreamstime.com: 3drenderings (r). 31 123RF.com: alein

(ca). Dreamstime.com: Dule964 (Leaves). 32 Dreamstime. com: Sergei Razvodovskij / Snr (cla). 33 123RF.com: Oksana Tkachuk (cra); wklzzz (br). Dorling Kindersley: Paolo Mazzei (cb). Dreamstime.com: Isselee (c). 34-35 Dreamstime .com: Inga Nielsen / Inganielsen. 35 Dreamstime.com: Designprintck (Background). 36 Dorling Kindersley: Stephen Oliver (b). 40 123RF.com: neydt (bl). 41 123RF.com: avtg (clb). 42-43 123RF.com: Ralph Schmaelter (Davidia involucrata). Dreamstime.com: Designprintck (Paper). 44 Alamy Stock Photo: Historic Collection (clb); Universal Images Group North America LLC / DeAgostini (l). Dreamstime.com: Alexander Potapov (tc). 45 Alamy Stock Photo: Blickwinkel (tr). 46 123RF.com: Steven Prorak (cl). 46-47 iStockphoto.com: Orbon Alija. 48-49 Dreamstime. com: Designprintck (b). 50-51 Alamy Stock Photo: Mint Images Limited. 51 Dreamstime.com: Designprintck (Background). 52 Dorling Kindersley: Kim Taylor (cla); Jerry Young (cra); Paolo Mazzei (bc). 52-53 123RF.com: Andrzej Tokarski / ajt (cb). Dreamstime.com: Dule964 (b/Leaves). 53 123RF.com: Steve Byland / steve_byland (cla/Sapsucker); Eric Isselee / isselee (ca); wklzzz (cl). Dorling Kindersley: British Wildlife Centre, Surrey, UK (cr); Natural History Museum, London (cla); Paolo Mazzei (cla). Dreamstime.com: Alle (cla/Bee); Jessamine (ca/Nest); Jim Cumming (cb). 54 Dorling Kindersley: Natural History Museum, London (cla); Andy and Gill Swash (clb). SuperStock: Glenn Bartley / All Canada Photos (cra). 55 123RF.com: Michael Zysman / deserttrends (cr). Alamy Stock Photo: Amazon-Images (c/ Ant); Andrew Barker (ca); Life on White (br). Dorling Kindersley: Thomas Marent (ca/Pitcher Plant); Jerry Young (fcl, c/Leopard); Natural History Museum, London (fbr). Dreamstime.com: Eric Isselee (c/Marmoset, cb); Pablo Hidalgo / Pxhidalgo (tc); Matthijs Kuijpers (cra). Getty Images: Martin Harvey / Photodisc (c). 56 Alamy Stock Photo: imageBROKER (c). Dreamstime.com: Philip Bird (crb); Vivian Mcaleavey (cla); William Bode (clb); Musat Christian / Musat (cb); Jnjhuz (clb/Beaver). 57 123RF.com: Mariusz Jurgielewicz (br). Alamy Stock Photo: imageBROKER (fclb, clb). Dorling Kindersley: Booth Museum of Natural History, Brighton (cla). Dreamstime.com: Gunold Brunbauer / Gunold (cr). 58 Dorling Kindersley: Greg and Yvonne Dean (tc). Dreamstime.com: Feathercollector (cr); Trubavin (cra); Mikhail Blajenov / Starper (clb). 59 Dorling Kindersley: Greg and Yvonne Dean (ca); Jerry Young (ob); Andy and Gill Swash (cl). Dreamstime.com: Chatchawin Pola / Chatchawin (clb); Suradech (c). 60 123RF.com: Maksym Bondarchuk (cla, cra); zerbor (cra/Silver birch). Dreamstime.com: Gunold Brunbauer / Gunold (fcrb); Josefpittner (tc); Steve Byland / Stevebyland (clb); Vanessa Gifford / Vanessagifford (crb). 61 123RF.com: belchonock (c/Tree); zerbor (cla, ca/Silver birch, fclb/Silver birch); Maksym Bondarchuk (ca, cra, cb); liligraphie (c); fotoplanner (cr, c/Fir tree); mediagram (c/Pine trees). Dreamstime.com: Helen Panphilova / Gazprom (clb); Horia Vlad Bogdan / Horiabogdan (fclb); Moose Henderson / Visceralimage (clb/Pine Martine); Scattoselvaggio (bc). 62 Alamy Stock Photo: imageBROKER (clb). 63 Fotolia: Eric Isselee (cl, fcl); Steve Lovegrove (clb). 64-65 123RF.com: ronstik. 65 Dreamstime.com: Designprintck (Background). 66 Dreamstime.com: Grafner (tl); Valentyn75 (crb). 67 123RF.com: Akulamatiau (clb); sunteya (cl); Gabor Havasi (tc); Karandaev (ca); Malosee Dolo (cb/Bottle). Dreamstime.com: Isabel Poulin (bl); Roman Samokhin (cb). 68 123RF.com: Katarzyna Białasiewicz (fcr/Table chair); serezniy (cra); Turgay Koca (fcr); Sakarin Plangson (ca); wklzzz (l). Dreamstime.com: Pictac (cr). 68-69 123RF.com: wklzzz (bc). 69 123RF.com: George Tsartsianidis (tc); wklzzz (r). Dreamstime .com: Dmitry Rukhlenko / F9photos (bc); Piotr Adamowicz / Simpson333 (cla). Fotolia: sisna (bl). 70 Dreamstime.com: Ruslan Nassyrov / Ruslanchik (bl). 72-73 Dreamstime.com: Designprintck

(Background). 74-75 Dreamstime.com: Designprintck (Background). 75 Dreamstime.com: Andrzej Tokarski (c). 76-77 Dreamstime.com: Designprintck (Background). 76 123RF.com: joseelias (bc); Valentyn Volkov (tc). 77 123RF.com: fotoplanner (tc). 78-79 Dreamstime.com: Designprintck (Background). 80 Dreamstime.com: Designprintck (Background)

Cover images: Front: 123RF.com: Eric Isselee / Isselee clb, c, Yuliia Sonsedska / sonsedskaya cb/ (Raccoon); **Dorling Kindersley:** British Wildlife Centre, Surrey, UK cb, crb, RHS Wisley; **Back:** 123RF.com: Eric Isselee / Isselee c; **Dorling Kindersley:** Paradise Park, Cornwall cla, RHS Wisley; **Fotolia:** Eric Isselee cl

All other images © Dorling Kindersley

ABOUT THE ILLUSTRATOR

Claire McElfatrick is a freelance artist. She created illustrated greetings cards for 12 years before working on children's books. Her illustrations for *The Magic & Mystery of Trees* are inspired by her home in rural England. Her artwork is a mix of hand-drawn illustration, collage, and digital techniques.